JOKES AND PUNS FOR GROAN-UPS

by

James T. Moore & Peter R. Chaston

Live well + Laugh often

Jim Moore

Chaston Scientific, Inc.
P.O. Box 758
Kearney, MO 64060
phone: 816-628-4770
fax: 816-628-9975

Library of Congress Catalog Card Number: 96-71116

ISBN: 0-9645172-3-X

DEDICATION

Jim Moore would like to dedicate this book to his mother, Alice Moore, who always believed in him, his loving wife, Kathy, who has patiently endured his puns over the years and nevertheless stands by him, his Uncle Jack Zeller, who taught him how to laugh, and to his colleagues and students, who have endured groaning up with him. Thank you, everyone! Jim's motto is, "We have to grow old, but we don't have to grow up!"

Pete Chaston dedicates this book to his loving wife, Mary, and loving daughter, Valerie, who more-or-less understand his sense of humor. Pete also dedicates this book to the <u>thousands</u> of people he has inflicted jokes, puns, quips and funny stories upon over the years! Pete's motto is, "A little nonsense now and then, is relished by the wisest men and women."

Although many of the jokes, puns, etc. in this book are original, many others were told to us over the years by friends, colleagues, students and others. Their anonymity is probably good for them, which allows us to take the groans for these quips. We therefore also express an appreciative thank-you to everyone else whose humor contributes to this book!

TABLE OF CONTENTS

Note: none of these jokes may be told or reproduced without the expressed written consent of the authors or someone else.

INTRODUCTION

JAMES T. (JIM) MOORE and **PETER R. (PETE) CHASTON** are both professional meteorologists. Jim Moore earned his Ph.D in Meteorology from Cornell University and Pete Chaston earned his M.S. in Meteorology from the University of Wisconsin, while under a National Weather Service Fellowship. How is it that two people with scientifically technical backgrounds, who have written books about weather and published numerous research articles, would end up co-authoring a pun and joke book?

HOW THIS BOOK CAME ABOUT

Well, both weathermen are well-known in the weather world for mixing humor with science. Jim started his puntastic career in junior high, cracking wise (but many times unwise) about the teacher or the subject they were discussing. Hey, if puns were good enough for Shakespeare, who could argue with their place in history? Jim Moore has been teaching meteorology at Saint Louis University in St. Louis, Missouri for over 16 years. He has been know to inject jokes and puns into his lectures at the University and talks given to various religious and civic groups and grade schools. Pete's weather forecasts and jokes made him a media celebrity when he did radio weather shows. Then for 13 years he trained National Weather Service forecasters to forecast, while also subjecting them to many of the jokes, quips and puns that are now incorporated into this book. His humor also spills over onto his popular program on Kansas City radio, "The Pete Chaston Doo-Wop Show", on which he plays 1950's-60's-style records by doo-wop shoo-bop groups.

We feel quite lucky to be able to work with the English language, which adapts beautifully to our "punsmanship". In fact, most languages, to the authors' knowledge, generally do not lend themselves to this type of word play. We are indeed fortunate to have such a rich language, some words of which your teacher never torture in school! Remember don't attempt to do this at home, we are trained professionals who know how to bend the English language to our bidding and are used to the abuse that ensues from a groaning audience. If you attempt this at home, you may lose friends, be disinherited from wills and basically live the rest of your life in isolation. Pete and Jim spent many years in the "punitentiary" and know how to deal with the audiences' "booze" and tomatoes in the face.

Thus, these two contemporary meteorologists and "pungents", who incidentally both started punning with each other when they were at New York University in the Bronx, New York City in the early 1970s, collaborated on this adventure. So it has come to pass that after many years of inflicting these jokes and puns on other meteorologists and understanding friends and relatives, it was time to come out of the clouds and share their jokes and puns with the rest of the world! So here it is...JOKES AND PUNS FOR GROAN-UPS. Enjoy!

Above is a picture of Jim Moore and Pete Chaston each eating a piece of pizza. You might ask: "Well, then where's the pizza?" Well, they finished eating it. Then you might ask, "Well, then where are Pete and Jim?" Well, after they ate the pizza, there was no reason for them to stay, so they left!

FAMILY JOKES

The only thing worse than a flooded basement
is a flooded attic.

How many knees do you have? Answer: FIVE!:
right knee, left knee, 2 kid-neys and one hiney.

This employee kept jabbing his new boss on the shoulder with a toothpick. When the
boss asked the employee what was he doing, the employee remarked, "Oh, I just wanted
to make a good impression on you."

My neighbor pulled out his teeth so that he could have more gum to chew.

What has 16 feet and wears a bra? Answer: Snow White and the seven dwarfs.

The husband says to his wife, "My dear, you look rather melancholy tonight. You have
the head of a melon and the face of a collie."

A man runs into the police station shouting, "Help! Help! A man just stole my car!"
The police sergeant asked him, "Did you get a description of the thief?" "No," replied
the man, "but I got the license plate number!"

I left my last job because of back trouble. Yep, they told me that if I ever came back,
there'd be trouble.

Teacher to student: "Mikey, how do you spell 'weather'?"
Mikey: "W-E-D-D-E-R."
Teacher: "That's the worst spell of weather we've had around here in a long time!"

I asked my friend, "Why am I running around in circles?" He told me, "Shut up or I'll
nail your other foot to the floor!"

Always be sincere, whether you mean it or not.

All his life through age 6, little Mikey never talked...he just never said a word, no
matter how much coaxing his parents gave him. Finally, on his sixth birthday, his mom
gave him lamb chops and spinach to eat. Suddenly, little Mikey blurts out, "THIS
FOOD STINKS!" His startled mom said, "Why, Mikey! How come you haven't said
anything for all these years?" Mikey replied, "Well, up until now, everything's been
fine!"

She goes out with only the upper set. She keeps her lower set in a glass filled with water.

If your parents didn't have children, you won't either.

She: "Why is your first name, 'Exit'?"
He: "My parents wanted to see my name up in lights all across America."

I just had a pleasure trip: I drove my mother-in-law to the airport.

Definition of a "tropical depression": Saving your money for a year to take a vacation at Disney World, and while you're there it rains every day.

When my neighbor was born, he was so ugly, that the doctor slapped his mother.

The horse I bet on was really good! He was so good that it took seven horses to beat him!

Four expectant fathers, all afraid to be with their wives during childbirth, were anxiously awaiting the births of their children as they fidgeted around in the waiting room. A maternity nurse came into the room to the first father and said, "Congratulations! You're the father of twins!" The dad exclaims, "WOW! That's a neat coincidence, because I'm a pitcher for the Minnesota Twins!" A half-hour later, a maternity nurse comes into the waiting room to the second dad, and says, "Congratulations! Your wife just had triplets!" "WOW!", exclaimed the new dad, "That's quite a coincidence because I work for the 3-M Manufacturing Company!" About another half-hour later, a maternity nurse comes into the room and goes to the next dad and says, "And congratulations to you! You are the proud father of quadruplets!" This new dad says, "WOW! What a coincidence! I'm a singer in the vocal group, The Four Seasons!" Just then, the last expectant father got up and told the nurse, "I'm getting out of here! I work for Seven-Up!"

On the seventh day of the seventh month of the year, Mr. Jefferson had seven good friends over the house. They played seven hands of poker and he won all seven times. When his friends went home, he took a walk and found a wad of seven hundred dollar bills, So he decided to go to the race track and bet the seven-hundred dollars on the seventh race, betting on horse number seven. After the race, he went home, and Mrs. Jefferson asked him, "Well, how did your horse do at the races?" "Well," he told her, "he came in seventh."

Well, you know about diesel engines. At the factory, my neighbor used to install these engines into trucks. He was a DIESEL FITTER. Then, after his plant laid him off, he got a job managing a shoe store. He told me he's still a diesel fitter. When a lady customer comes in and asks for a pair of shoes, he pulls a set out and says, "diesel fitter".

My cousin was always complaining that his head hurts. So, finally I told him, "Remember, when you get out of bed, it's FEET first!"

A lady goes into a delicatessen and tells the clerk, "I want a pound of kidelly beans, please." The clerk says, "What? Would you repeat that, please." The lady says, "I'd like a pound of kidelly beans!" The clerk then says, "What's that, again? What do you want?" The lady says again, "I'd like a pound of kidelly beans!" The clerk then says, "Oh!, You mean you want a pound of KIDNEY beans!" She says, "Yes, kidelly beans. That's what I said, diddle I?"

How did Webster create the dictionary? Answer: He got into a fight with his wife, and one word led to another.

Did you hear about the mother flea who got upset because all her kids were going to the dogs?

My neighbor used to work in a bubble gum factory, and once he fell into a vat of bubble gum. Boy, did his boss chew him out!

My neighbor looked up his family tree and discovered that he was the sap.

My buddy's girlfriend is so sweet, that you could catch diabetes just standing next to her.

My neighbor's wife is a light eater. Every time it gets light outside, she starts eating.

I had a light breakfast this morning.
I ate a 100-watt bulb.

My neighbor took an extra shoe to the golf course, in case he got a hole in one.

The first girl I proposed to said NO! But she then said, "but I admire your good choice in women!"

I asked my neighbor, "Do you have trouble making up your mind?" He replied, "Well, yes and no."

There's a lot of apathy around here, but who cares?

I stopped at a "School Crossing" sign and waited all day, but didn't see one school go by.

I took my umbrella to work and it started to rain. When I opened it, it was full of holes so I got wet. My co-worked said to me, "Why did you take the umbrella with the holes in it?" I told him, "I didn't think it was going to rain."

Knock, knock.
Who's there?
Sensuous.
Sensuous who?
Sensuous such a nice person, here are some more jokes.

Knock, knock.
Who's there?
Little old lady.
Little old lady who?
I didn't know you could yodel.

My neighbor gets so many parking tickets that the police department just issued him a season's ticket.

Tourist to local person: Have you lived your whole life here?
Local person: No, not yet.

NEWSFLASH: A guy just walked through a screen door! He strained himself.

A lady had two tattoos on her knees. She had the devil tattooed on one knee and fire on the other. When she crossed her legs, it looked like hell.

Father to son: "Son, what do you dream about?"
Son: "Football!"
Father: Football?"
Son: "Yes, football."
Father: "Why don't you dream about something else, such as girls, cars?"
Son: "What! and miss the kick-off?!"

My word processor is messing up. When I type a letter, such as "I", I get two of that letter, and when a type a number, such as "2", I get two of that number. So I called the software company up and their representative told me, "Well, you know the old saying, 'An i for an i and a 2 for a 2'."

My neighbor said she just made a cake with honey; it's good to see her husband help!

Neighbor: "My dog is lost!"
Me: "Put an ad in the paper."
Neighbor: "That's no good. My dog can't read."

I went on a two-week diet...and lost 14 days.

My next door neighbor just invented unscented perfume.

Did you ever notice that no matter what temperature a room is, it's always room temperature?

My next door neighbor once dated a belly dancer. But she dropped him. She claimed he turned her stomach.

Here's my best friend: good ole what's-his-name.

Patience is a virtue;
Polyester is a fabric.

There's a new organization called "DAM". It's the "Mothers Against Dyslexia."

The coldest weather I ever experienced was a summer in Duluth.

We two writers of this book stayed up all last night to see where the sun went when it set. And then it dawned on us!

I'm not saying my neighbor was feeling down in the dumps, but last night his cat tried to bury him in the kitty litter.

You certainly have a way with words, and how you get away with those words, I'll never know.

A neighbor was a guest at the house of a new couple in the neighborhood. He had to go use the restroom. Suddenly, the neighbor yells out, "There's no toilet paper!" The host yells back, "Then use a dollar!" About five minutes later, the neighbor comes back from the bathroom with blood dripping down his leg. The host asks, "What happened?" The neighbor told him, "I did what you suggested. I used four quarters."

Then there was the lazy guy who married a pregnant woman.

He's a legend in his own mind; his reputation exceeds him.

A man fell off the Empire State Building. A cop runs over to him and asks, "What happened?" The man replies, "I don't know; I just got here myself."

It's handy to have fingers.

Man to adversary: "I like a man of conviction, and you ought to be convicted."

Here is how you get ahead in life: It's not WHO you know, but WHOM you know!

Teacher: Bobby, spell "Mississippi".
Bobby: The river or the state?

I asked the campus security department to beef up security around our offices, so they sent us fat cops.

The newspaper said that the city was planning on building nightclubs and gambling casinos on the old bridge crossing the Mississippi River. Great idea, but how are they going to keep the Bridge Over the River Quiet?

A woman was taking her husband to court as he was so stingy he wouldn't give her money to buy a new bra. She was suing him for lack of support.

My friend is so lazy he got his birthmark when he was 12.

The woman lawyer was so fat she had to incorporate herself.

Our mailman is too old for his job. He lost a little bit of his zip.

I like our new mailman. He carries his job out to the letter.

My neighbor was planning to build a fence and asked for my help. I told him to keep me posted.

My friend is so stupid. He only plays his AM radio in the morning.

I took my shoes to the shoemaker to put new heels on them.
He soled them instead.

Boy, did I lace into him; but the shoe was fit to be tied.

I asked for a dozen clams and six oysters at the seafood restaurant. Perhaps I was a little shellfish. But the waiter didn't crab. He said that it was no fluke to order so much fish (so he told the tail). I was not ashamed. No way was I going to flounder in front of him and look stupid.

We finally found a secretary who could work with our new computer and do word processing. Her name is Dot Matrix.

A sign in front of the mortuary said, "Join our funeral plan now! We'll be the last ones to let you down."

The sports store advertised that it was having a sale on tennis balls. "First come, first serve", the sign read.

A new beauty salon opened up at the mall near us. It's called the "Curl Up and Dye". Actually, the beauty shop had a catch slogan that said, "If your hair isn't becoming to you, you ought to be coming to us".

I needed cash so I went to the bank asking for the Loan Arranger but the teller sent me to Tonto.

The course that I took on river flooding was over my head. Left me high and dry. The instructor had a punk hair style. I guess he was new wave.

I've had a falling out with my barber. He said, "How long do you want over the ears? Half inch or so?". "Let's not split hairs;" I told him, "after all, my hair is the last thing I care to part with."

Replacing fluorescent fixtures is really light work.
I told that to our repairman at work and he blew his fuse.

A poor business to go into is the umbrella business. Too much overhead.

My friend was a great violin player but had to quit after 5 years. He was all strung out. Apparently fretted too much.

My town is so small they only have a town triangle.

I went over to the sales clerk holding a pair of suspenders and said, "This is a hold up".

"Is there turbulence?", the pilot shouted, "Why, it is so bad up here I have white caps on my coffee!"

<u>Things that you hear that are not true</u>:
- I've never done this with anyone else before.
- This won't hurt much at all.
- Your car will be ready by noon.
- We sent that check to you last week.
- Oh, funny thing that you called because I have your file right on my desk.
- I was looking at your car claim right now.
- Sure we put new parts in the your car when we repair it.
- I guarantee that the odometer on this baby hasn't been turned back.
- And we'll even deliver this furniture to your home for free!
- We real don't make money on these maintenance contracts, you know.

So I told the girl that my mother was a midget. After all I was much better at small talk.

When he hit his foot against the bed
he cried in pain. So I called a toe truck.

Quasimoto. Does that name ring a bell?

After horsing around with the gymnast I showed him the ropes.

"Michelangelo", the Pope lamented, "next time use a roller!"

Forecast for Indian summer. Warm days and cool nights with a chance for Apache fog in the valleys.

Sign on Swimming Pool store: Save Big Money on Our Liquidation Sale!

I went to a store that had a sale. The sign read: All jeans half off. They were selling shorts!

The tree doctor down the street is doing such a good business that he opened up a branch office.

The PBS station had a special on the danger of flash floods. I didn't understand it. Most of the material was over my head.

Just the other day my wife took me to go shopping and malled me.

I didn't want to buy a rug from the salesman at the carpet store. He had no tack.

A plumber bent over to pick up a lead pipe and one of his tools fell on him. Now he says he's wrenched his back.

I don't have my watch worked on by that jeweller anymore. Last time he charged me too much and ticked me off.

My friend is a sore loser at golf. I don't play with him once he's teed off. Besides he always cheats. Never plays the fairway.

That secretary was not my type.

The glazer fell on a window. Now he's a pain in the glass.

A guy jogging came upon a buxom girl jogging as well. When he met up with her he called out that classic line, "My pace or yours?"

I'm not into the health scene these days. The only thing I do is jog my memory and wrestle with my conscience. Heck, weight lifting for me is getting out of my easy chair.

Golfers always are looking for plush fairways and the perfect putting green. They think that the greens are grassier on the other clubs.

I saw a sign on a garbage truck the other day saying, "Our business is picking up."

I go to the dry cleaner only when I'm hard pressed for a clean shirt.

It is difficult to navigate near Alaska. It's not easy to keep your Bearings Strait.

In Alaska if you look to the west some people say you can Russia but I believe its only an Aleutian.

I got mugged the other day. The guy hit my nose and now it looks crooked. I sued the mugger for deformation of character.

A beautiful woman was also a brilliant chemistry professor. She needed a date for Friday so I gave her Avagadros' number.

The people of Panama were ecstatic when the U. S. gave them rights over the canal. "Isthmus be our lucky day", the president shouted to the people.

How does the man in the moon get his hair cut? Eclipse it himself.

"How did you realize that the bell-ringer for the church was the killer?", the young detective asked his boss. "Oh, I had a hunch back at the office", his boss replied.

What is black and brown and looks good on a lawyer?
A doberman pincher.

Cosmeticians get through school easily since they are allowed to take makeup exams.

A tornado took the roof off the local hardware store yesterday. The owner started selling everything for half price today. I asked him why everything was so cheap. He said, "It's easy selling things cheap when you have no overhead!".

The young student exhibited his science fair project at the local fair. He had different D cells in a flashlight to see which brand was the best buy. One could say that he ran a battery of tests.

I heard that a bus load of convicts being transferred to another prison ran into a concrete truck on the highway yesterday. Fortunately, no one got hurt but the state police are looking for twenty hardened criminals.

I'm so scared of heights that I didn't even use Cliff notes in high school.

Her cooking is so bad pygmies drop by to dip their darts in her soup.

He is so skinny he has to run around in a shower to get wet.

He is so fat he leaves pot holes behind him on the sidewalk.

He is on a seafood diet. Every time he sees food he eats it.

I'm getting that furniture look. My chest is dropping into my drawers.

He got so fat his bellybutton turned from an "innee" into an "outee".

I always get diarrhea after eating at the hamburger joint. Sort of gives new meaning to the term "fast food".

His stomach has moved out to where the vest begins.

Group dieters could always form a weighting pool.

A string walks into a bar and ask the bartender for a drink.
The bartender says, "Hey, buddy aren't you a string?".
"Well, yes, I am. What about it?", the string replies.
The bartender says, "Well, we don't serve drinks to string!".
The string stomps out of the bar. Outside he ruffles up his
top and then walks back into the bar. "Hey, aren't you the
string that I just kicked out of here?", the bartender says
to the string.
"NO, I'm a frayed knot!".

The only way that he can lower his weight is by sitting on the floor.

I knew a guy who worked from 9 to 5 for the government; he was a shiftless worker.

There is a division within the police department now to investigate computer-related
theft. The cops want to take a byte out of crime.

They used to run a miniature golf-course and made a lot of money on it. But now they
are in the hole.

Being a plumber can be a draining job; being a locksmith can be a boring job.

Mattress salesmen are laid back.

Bored bank tellers usually lose interest.

I was baffled by the waterbed salesman.

The carpenter had a cutting sense of humor.

The dentist enjoyed biting sarcasm. But most of his jokes were tongue in cheek.

He was bald at an early age. Even in High School he was nominated as "most likely to recede".

The ventriloquist threw his voice and hurt his neck.

subtitle: Name of a U-boat.

A man walks along a dock counting the openings between the boards until he falls into the water. Moral: When you're out of slits you're out of pier.

The NFL football players were going to play a team made up of prison inmates. The game was advertised as the "Pros vs. Cons".

The man next door finally got rid of the bugs on his scalp but he got a ticket from the local cops for driving without head lice.

A cartographer is a man who knows where to draw the line.

I had to return my jogging suit to the athletic store... I wore it only once and it had a run in it.

International date line: Hey, baby how about going to a movie with me?

Sign by a music store: Gone Chopin, Bach in a Minuet.

populate: what mom says to dad when he comes back from playing poker with his friends.

subscribe: the undersecretary of the Navy.

Most people were scared by the tsunami but he thought that it was swell.

vulgar: a river in Russia.

subside: the port or starboard flank of a u-boat.

My friend used to work for a computer software company until they gave him the boot.

Man at bar: Give me a glass of prune juice.
Bartender: Is that for here?
Man at bar: No, it's to go.

treason: what the acorn is to the tree.

He wanted to buy the Indian carvings but he didn't know how to totem home.

I want to be the spokesperson for
a bicycle company.

The electrician's fears were not grounded.

A midget clairvoyant escapes from prison.
The newspaper headline read: Small medium at large.

I couldn't sleep under the stars due to the noise in the Sonoran Desert.
I saw a baseball player get hit between the legs by a baseball.
He didn't cry because he was a groin man.

I had a flat while driving my car to work. I decided to retire.

I saw a couple of geologists today going out for shakes. They were very gneiss people,
but you can't take them for granite.

The people from NASA are really hip. One of the guys came up to me and said,
"Hey, lets do launch!".

Do artists ever get framed?

Do golfers ever play the fairway?

Have you ever seen a bathroom sink?
A woman who just gave birth to quadruplets, named them Eenie, Meenie, Miney and
Frank. Her husband said, "Why Frank?", to which she replied, "because I didn't want
any Moe!"

Did you ever see a plumber twist a wrench too hard and faucet?

My friend complained that he hadn't had a date in weeks. I gave him a calendar.

The shoe store salesmen were a couple of loafers.

I took my first date for a car ride. We paused near a YIELD sign and she did.

The ambulance had "Patient Transportation" printed on it but the driver sped impatiently along the street with his lights flashing.

I believe that the Navy sank three ships but frankly I frigate.

Abacuses are easy to use once you get a bead on it.

The man wanted to cross the river but there was no bridge.
So I called him a ferry but he slapped me!

I lit my lighter for the man for his cigar but before I got to him he had met his match.

The blacksmith signed the check and was charged with forgery.

The composer could not control the orchestra even though he gave the job his concerted effort. He sure had the audiences' symphonies.

I parked my car at the mall and an attendant said to me, "That was a great job of parking". The stores were offering complimentary parking.

The artist went to school for 5 years but never finished collage.

The secretary thought that she was being elite but I was not font of her.

The judge was a man of conviction so he handed the English professor a long sentence for passing a red light.

He is a very well-balanced man, he has a chip on both shoulders.

Wyatt Earp was the right caliber man for the job.

We buried him near a rose bush since he was a blooming idiot.

We had to remove the Air Force stickers that were in the men's room. AIM HIGH is not a good motto over the urinals.

Outpatient: A person that has fainted.

The prospective cheerleader got the job since he had a leg up on the competition.

Did you know that the inventor of the door knocker got the Nobel prize?

A few of us were tired sitting on the bar stools all night but Guy LeFranc was feeling fine. He said that he had studied for years at the Sore Bun.

A movie projectionist must be screened before he gets the job.

When Iowans get sick they know how Dubuque.

Going out with everyone in Ohio: Dayton, OH.

Spooky city in PA: Erie, PA.

When a mortician is not paid for his services, he gets stiffed.

If one perfume smells like another can we say that it has been cologned? Who gives two scents anyway?

Fungi: Life of the party.

What vegetable is a drummer's favorite? Beets.

When an altar boy is too nervous on the job he burns the candle at both ends.

Did you hear about the morning after pill for men? It changes your blood type.

I got a call the other day from an amoeba. He used his cellular phone.

I was once a friend of a midget until he belittled me.

If you don't pay your exorcist on time you can get repossessed.

I was thrown out of the concert hall because I didn't conduct myself.
The violinist was kicked out of the orchestra pit for passing notes. He had eaten his music.

She didn't know what color to pick. Blue, red, green, fusche.
So she decided to go back to the fusche.

Both father and son wore the same colored sweaters made by mom. They were a close knit family.

The origami store folded.

The plumbing service went down the tubes.

The dry cleaner lost his shirt.

The elevator repairman got the shaft.

I went to see the movie, "Awakenings", and fell asleep.

The physicists tried to woo his girlfriend. He said to her,
"Would you care to dyne with me?" After dinner her asked for her hand in marriage and showed her a large joule.

Stinky's cesspool cleaner: We are number 1 in the number 2 business.

The oil companies don't hire people unless they are doing well.

The Dean of the Arts and Sciences college heard that several of the professors were going to take early retirement. He was concerned that he was losing his faculties.

The students did not like the cafeteria food. They said that they were fed up with it.

Do carpenters ever get board?

I asked for the shoe shine man to shine my boots, but I was rebuffed.

When the customer complained to the car mechanic about his work he got jacked off.

The New York Yankees after "The Babe" retired: Ruthless.

The farmer went to the dentist for treatment for his sorghum.

The destitute fisherman tried to steal a box of laundry detergent but was caught before he went out with the tide.

apparent: Mom or Dad.

transparent: Mom is Dad.

Guy: Will I see you pretty soon?
Girlfriend: What's the matter?
Don't you think I'm pretty now?!

I stuck my head up the chimney and caught the flue.

Did you hear about the Mexican fireman whose wife had twins?
They named them Hose A and Hose B.

Mother: My little Johnny has grown 4 inches this past year.
Storekeeper: Yes, I noticed that he's grewsome.

I opened up my paycheck and found parsley in the envelope.
Apparently, my wages had been garnished.

Do you prefer to go cycling with friends?
No, I prefer to cyclone.

My mother told me not to worry about meeting a girl. She said that there were plenty of fish in the sea. But I worried to myself, Do I lack allure?

I took a lie detector test.
No, I didn't.

A Chinese American who immigrated to the United States not too long ago, was in line to obtain his first driver's license. The man behind the desk said, "Next!" The Chinese man went up to him to get his driver's license. The following conversation ensued.
Clerk: "What is your name please?"
Chinese man: "Thaddeus Kluzewski."
The clerk looked up at the man.
Clerk: "You're Chinese. Is this some kind of joke?"
Chinese man: "No, it isn't. My named is Thaddeus Kluzewski."
Clerk: "Do you mind my asking you this, how an American citizen from a Chinese ethnic background got the name, Thaddeus Kluzewski?"
Chinese man: "Well, when a bunch of us new immigrants were at the immigration station entering this country, the man before me was named Thaddeus Kluzewski, and when the immigration official who was filling out the papers asked him his name, he told the official he was Thaddeus Kluzewski."
Clerk: "So then what happened?"
Chinese man: "Well, next it was my turn. Without looking up to see me, the immigration man aked me my name, so I told him: Sam Ting."

PAGE 19

Why did Cleopatra refuse to accept that Mark Athony had left her?
She was Queen of Denial.

Diatribe: American Indians on slim-fast.

Sky divers are good to the last drop.

Don't let your karma run over my dogma.

He had a swelled head and capsized.

Secant: dyslexic blind man.

Sign in Hot Air balloon store: Buy now before inflation!

I just can't grow flowers in my garden", Tom said lackadaisically.

rutabaga: an obnoxious panhandler.

franchise: food served best with hamburgers.

concave: hideout for escaped prisoners.

A beard can look scruffy at first, but after a while it grows on you.

marionette: what Frankie Avalon wanted to do.

It takes so long to fly to China that most people need time to get oriented.

penultimate: the greatest writing instrument.

postulate: when letters are mailed after 3 p.m.

bratwurst: most ill-behaved child in class.

magazine for gardeners: weeder's digest.

Did Tennessee the same thing that Arkansas? Guess Alaska and find out what Juneau.

Wedding: an event that always comes off with a hitch.

Coach: Son, can you pass this football?
Walk on: Gee, coach, I can barely swallow it!

Toupee in Japan: an oriental rug.

What sound does a piano make when it falls down a mine shaft? A flat minor.

My barber and I had a fight. Now we are shorn enemies.

I am an incorrigible punster. Please don't incorrige me.

The painter drank more and more turpentine until he simply varnished into thin air.

She was so ugly that when she walked into the bank the security cameras were turned off.

I went over to the beautiful cashier and checked her out.

I like to bowl --
in my spare time.

Cantaloupe: What the father said to the young man upon seeing him with a ladder outside his daughter's room.

How did the ice form on the wings of the jet? There appeared to be no rime or reason.

"I can put the stitches in myself", said the boastful intern.
His mentor replied, "Okay, suture self."

I burned the midnight oil with an old flame.

I'm no genus at classifying animals.

What's a metaphor if you can't use it?

The amoeba was funny but of the one celled organisms, the paramecium was cilia.

mirage: an optical delusion.

The mathematician enjoyed sunbathing and he was a tan gent. He did sneeze a lot, especially in the Spring since he had trouble with his sine xs.

natural logarithm: in-born singing/dancing ability of woodsmen.
Pedicure: What a veterinarian does.

Person who wishes to perform about C level should study on a mountain top.

She ran into the fabric outlet, grabbed the blue fabric and bolted out the door.

imaginary number: what a mathematician tells you if you ask him his age.

overcast: when too many people are chosen for the lead role.

thaw: past tense of "tsee".

fog bank: when the cost of writing a check is not clear.

I went on dates with so many women in Ohio, I felt like I was Dayton, OH.
But none were the Marion type.

Is Casper, Wyoming a ghost town?

News Headline in Iowa: Indian hit by bus - tries to Sioux City.

I held my wedding reception in Illinois and Decatur took care of all the food planning.

Most boring airport in the U.S.: Dulles Airport, Washington, D.C.

Not all the airports in Idaho are small potatoes. At least one of their cities is usually Boise.

In England would fog ever be mist?

I know my supper is ready when the smoke alarm goes off.

Billy came home from school and said to his parents, "MOM!, DAD! I got 100 in two subjects!" "Why, that's wonderful!", responded his mother. His father then asked, "Which two subjects, son?" Billy replied, "A 60 in English and a 40 in Math!"

What do you call a girl who has three boyfriends all named William? Answer: a Bill collector.

Here comes my weekend forecast
  for Jims and Janes and Floyds.
It either is a good one
  or one that's for the boids.

It will be cold this weekend,
  so wear some heavy clothes.

And if you do not like my poem,
  then shove it up your nose.

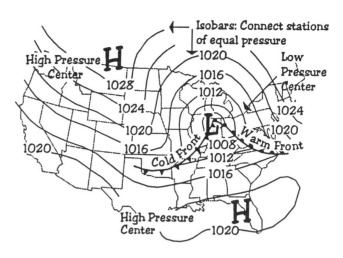

Did you hear about the Texan who put ice-cream on his head? He wanted to "Remember the A-la-mode."

Why, when the lady clapped her hands, did they make the sound, "clang, clang, clang" instead of "clap, clap, clap"? Answer: because she had dish-pan hands.

What language is Spokane in Washington state?

When I am fishing, I'm always catching books: telephone books, cookbooks, etc. So I wrote to an angler's magazine asking for advice. They asked me what kind of worms I was using. I told them, "Why, bookworms, of course!"

My new girlfriend is overly materialistic. While walking past a jewelry store, she exclaimed, "Why, I want that diamond necklace!" So I took out a brick from my coat and smashed the window to get the necklace for her. A few blocks later we passed a fur store, and she remarked, "I just love that cozy mink coat! If you truly love me, get it for me!" So I reached into my coat pocket, took out another brick, broke the store window and grabbed the fur coat to give it to her. A few blocks later, we're passing a new car dealership and she saw a flashy red sports car in the window. She said, "Why, darling, I just have to have that sports car" By now, enough was enough. I turned to her and cried out, "What do you think I am --- made out of bricks?!"

Why do we drive on parkways and park on driveways?

I was juggling three pocket dictionaries last night. Suddenly I lost my juggling rhythm and, since I had my mouth open, one of the dictionaries fell right into my mouth and down my throat. My friends pounded on my back, turned me upside down, and tried everything else they could think of to get me to cough it up...but they couldn't get a word out of me.

I asked my neighbor, "What were the most important ten years in your life?"
He replied, "High school."

A lady was looking to buy a thermometer to hang outside under her porch. She finally picked one out that said "Fahrenheit thermometer". "I'll take it, " she told the salesman, "that's a good brand."

A young lady was applying for her first secretarial job. In the job interview, the personnel clerk told her, "Well, this job pays $300 a week, but in six months the pay is $350." "Fine," said the applicant, "I'll come back in six months."

A sixth-grader came home with his report card which showed an A in spelling, an A in reading and an A in grammar. The mom knew her son wasn't that bright, so she went to visit the teacher. She told him, "You know, I'm not complaining that my son has straight A's in English, but I know he can't write well, he doesn't know how to spell big words, and he can't even express himself in a full sentence." The teacher replied to her, 'Oh well, that don't matter none nohow."

Grandfather to his grandson: "When you get to be my age, there are two important things that you should always have: first, your memory; second, I don't remember."

My friend checked his family tree and found out he was the sap.

My neighbor had so many pimples on his face when he was a teenager, that his mother used his face for a washboard.

What did Napoleon do with his little armies? Answer: He put them in his little sleevies.

Two trees were trying to do their algebra homework. One tree says to the other, "This problem has me stumped."

There's a lot of apathy in this office, but I just don't care.

1st dodo-head: "What do you have in that sack?"
2nd dodo-head: "Chickens! Guess how many and I will give you either of them."
1st dodo-head: "Three!"

Here is a story I (Pete C.) used to inflict on my meteorologist students when I taught at the National Weather Service Training Center:

My first job was a temporary summer job as an assistant forest ranger at Glacier National Park in northwest Montana. My first assignment was to follow a map given me, and hike several miles through the woods to find an old set of cabins that used to be used for hikers to stay in overnight. These fifty-year old cabins were going to be reopened, and my assignment was to find the cabins, remove the old rusty and moldy 50-year old locks on them, and replace them with new locks. So I hiked through the woods for a few hours, following my map, and eventually reached the cabins. Sure enough, the old locks were rusty and covered with mold. So I removed them, replacing them with the new locks, and put the old moldy ones back in my satchel. While walking through the woods I had a sense that something was following me. So I looked over my shoulder and say a big grizzly bear a short distance behind me. I didn't panic, although coming from the East Coast I did not know much about bears. The rangers told me to make noise, sink, etc. so that any grizzly bear I might encounter would know that I am a human and would leave me alone. So I started singing doo-wop songs, but the bear was still following me! A few minutes later I looked over my shoulder and there were now TWO grizzly bears! So I started to walk faster and faster. Then I looked over my shoulder again and say THREE grizzlies following me! By now I was starting to panic and ran to the first tree I though I could climb and climbed half-way up. I wasn't sure how well bears climbed trees. I looked down and saw the bears climbing up...they were tree bears; that is, they knew how to climb trees. Then I thought, "They know I'm a human; they can't be after me. It must be what's in my satchel!" So I opened the satchel and started throwing down the old moldy and rusty locks. Sure enough, the bears started licking all the tasty old mold off those locks. That is what they were after! And that is the story of "Moldy Locks and the Tree Bears".

A woman wanted to divorce her husband. So in court the judge asked her, "What are your grounds?" She replied, "oh, we have about three acres." The judge said, "That's not what I meant. Do you have a grudge?" She answered, "no, we don't have a garage, just a carport." The judge tried once more, "Lady, did he beat you up?" She replied, "No, I usually get up before he does." The exasperated judge then asked, "Lady, just tell me...why do you want a divorce?" She then told him, "My husband and I seem to have a problem communicating!"

We wrote down our best jokes and then threw the papers into the fireplace...and the fire just roared and roared!

I came home with a tulip, a carnation and a rose in my hair. My wife asked me what that was all about, to which I responded, "I just wanted to show who wears the plants in this family."

My neighbor, a farmer, has a pig with a wooden leg. I asked him how the pig got his wooden leg. He told me, "Well, one day I was changing a tire on my truck when the jack slipped and pinned my leg under the car. Well, my pig came up to me and with his wooden leg he raised the car so that I could get my leg out." I said, "That's quite a story, but it still doesn't explain HOW the pig got the wooden leg." So the farmer continued, "Well, one day I fell asleep on the couch and my cigar fell on the couch and started a fire. My pig smelled the smoke and ran up to the window. He kept tapping on the glass until he woke me and I put out the fire before it spread. My pig thus saved my life!" I replied, "That's a great story! But it still doesn't explain HOW your pig got his wooden leg!" Because of my insistence, the farmer then said to me, "O.K. Here's why my pig has a wooden leg. With a pig that good, you don't just eat him all at once."

My friend and I always wanted to be in a play on Broadway, so when we heard there were auditions for a play, we both jumped in his car and drove continuously from Missouri to New York City. My friend was so excited about being on Broadway that he accidentally stepped on the gas petal instead of the brake and we crashed through the side of a theater and landed in the middle of a stage where rehearsals were going on. The producer came to us, and I though about saying some wise-crack about "breaking into show business", but instead, when the producer of the play asked my friend who was driving, "What the heck do you think you're doing?", I responded, "Oh, you'll have to excuse my friend. It's just a stage he's going through!"

My neighbor claims he's a pilot. He picks it up here and piles it over there.

Why does Santa Claus have a garden? Answer: so he can hoe-hoe-hoe all summer!

My neighbor ran over himself. He asked me to get him donuts and I wouldn't, so he ran over himself.

While watching the great Hurricane Agnes flood as the raging waters of the Susquehanna River were going through Wilkes Barre, Pennsylvania, I was on one side of the river and the owner of a drug store was on the other side, nervously watching the rising waters threaten his drug store. The waters tore through a cemetery, and eerily, some caskets were floating past us. I yelled across to the druggist, "Hey! Do you have anything to stop this coffin?"

I need to take out a will. I'll call this law firm of Rabinowitz, Rabinowitz, Rabinowitz and Rabinowitz. "Hello, may I speak to Mr. Rabinowitz, please." "I'm sorry," the person who answered the phone replied, "but Mr. Rabinowitz is in court today." "Then may I speak with Mr. Rabinowitz?" "I'm sorry," he said, "but Mr. Rabinowitz is on the gold course this morning." "Then may I please speak with Mr. Rabinowitz?" "I'm sorry," he said, "but Mr. Rabinowitz is with a client right now." So I said, "Then may I please speak with Mr. Rabinowitz?" He replied, "Speaking."

What are two things you will never have for breakfast? Answer: lunch and supper.

What's the difference between a roll of toilet paper and loaf of bread? You don't know? Then I'd never send you to the grocery store to get a loaf of bread!

I used to work for a company that manufactured bullets. Yeah, I was a big shot. Unfortunately, they fired me. They said I wasn't the right caliber person for the job.

How may wives should a man have? Answer: sixteen; because when you get married, the priest/pastor/rabbi says, "Four better, four worse, four richer and four poorer"; so, four plus four plus four plus four equal sixteen! --sixteen wives!

Why is Ireland the fastest growing country in the world? Answer: its capital is always Dublin.

With my jokes, I'm the kind of person who brightens up a party by leaving it!

Well, you know what they say: scratch a man who looks like a turnip, and you'll have a man who looks like a scratched turnip.

Then there's this husband and wife team who are so unromantic that they call their water bed, "Lake Placid".

My brother is an only child.

An insult: "What do you think of the human race? I'd like the opinion of an outsider."

Avoid ending a sentence with a preposition; that is something up with which I will not put.

A freshman is walking on the grounds of Harvard. He stops a senior and asks, "Excuse me, can you tell me where the library is at?".
The senior replies snootily, "This is Harvard. We don't end our sentences with a preposition!"
"I'm sorry", says the freshman, "Can you tell me where the library is at, STUPID!"

When Sir Winston Churchill was having a debate with a female member of the opposition in Parliament, the argument got so intense that the woman blurted out, "Sir Winston, if I were your wife I'd put poison in your whiskey!", to which Sir Winston replied, "Madame, if I were your husband I would drink it!"

What's the name of that former lion tamer who always stuck his right hand into the lion's mouth? Answer: Lefty.

It was hereditary in my family to never have children.

I read the obituary page in the newspaper today. Did you know that everybody died in alphabetical order?

The lady down the road just lost 180 pounds: she divorced her husband.

Never jump out of an airplane without a parachute; you shouldn't jump to a conclusion.

My neighbor's basement got flooded with water. He was wearing one red sock and one blue sock. He got marooned.

My first girl-friend worked at a fast-food hamburger joint: they called her all-beef Patty.

Jack Spratt could eat no lean;
His wife could eat no fat.
And so between them
They ate the dog and cat.

Give me a sentence with the word "pencil" in it. Answer: "If you don't wear a belt, your pencil fall down!"

A family living in Vermont on the Vermont-Canadian border was just informed by the Canadian government that their property was mistakenly thought to be in Vermont for all these years, but after surveying was done, it was determined that this family lives on the Canadian side of the border. "Whew!", said the husband, "thank goodness! I couldn't take another of those Vermont winters!"

My uncle and aunt were in the iron and steal business. Yeah, my aunt irons and my uncle would steal.

My uncle's name was Ferdinand and my aunt's name was Liza, so they named their son Fertilizer.

My neighbor was in the hospital but he took a turn for the nurse.

People are more numerous in a crowd than when they are alone.

My neighbor wrote the entire Constitution of the United States on the head of a pin. Unfortunately, it was illegible.

Our local TV station interviewed a man who claims to be the oldest person in the world. When the reporter asked him if he could prove he was the oldest man, he replied, "Sure. I'll go to South America to get my grandfather who will swear to it."

I belong to the C.I.O.; everybody I see, I owe.

Do you know the Gettysburg Address? Answer: 23 Main Street; Gettysburg, Pennsylvania.

My friend is such a sore loser at golf; I just won't play with him once he's teed off!

Two drunks were walking through a cemetery. One fell into an open grave. He started saying, "Brrr, it's cold down here; brrr, it's cold down here." The second drunk heard this sound coming out of the hole, "Brrr, it's cold down here; brrr, it's cold down here." He staggered over to the hole and looked in, He saw the other drunk saying, "Brrr, it's cold down here; brrr, it's cold down here." The drunk looking down into the hole said, "No wonder you're cold; you done kicked all the dirt off ya!"

Never say, "Hi, Jack!" at an airport.

Pete: "I had a light breakfast this morning."
Jim: "What did you have?"
Pete: "A one hundred-watt bulb."

My high school classes were all on the top floor of the school; thus, I assured myself of getting a higher education.

I got stuck with my girlfriend in a revolving door, and we've been going around together ever since.

If you throw salt on your neighbor's car battery, you could be charged with a salt and battery.

A farmer let his young daughter date her new beaux. However, he warned the lad, "no hanky panky!" About 2 in the morning the farmer's wife heard the car drive up but a half hour later the daughter had still not come inside. So the wife whispered to her husband, "Sneak around outside and find out what they're doing in that car for so long." So the husband listened behind a car for a while and then snuck back inside. "Well," said the wife, "what are they doing?" "Oh, it's nothing," the farmer replied. "They're playing checkers." "CHECKERS?", cried the wife, "How do you know that?" The farmer told her, "Well, I heard her say to him, 'One more move like that and I'll crown you!' "

Why couldn't the pony sing? Answer: because he had a little colt. Why else couldn't the pony sing? Answer: because he was a little horse.

Marriage is a three ring ceremony: engagement ring, wedding ring and suffer-ring.

When Princess Di writes a book, does she collect royalties?

I saw a man in Kansas. He must have been a farmer. At least that was my overall impression.

My neighbor leady is so overweight that her driver license picture is an 8 1/2 by 11.

The man tried to jump over the iron fence but got stuck on the top of it.
He was overwrought.

I tried to jump my car the other day and hurt my knee on the roof.

FOOD JOKES & PUNS

A Cheeseburger walks into a bar.
"Sorry, but we don't serve food in here", says the bartender.

I went to a restaurant last night in a really tough neighborhood. I knew that it was a tough neighborhood because the waitress who served us had the menu tattooed on her arm.

Did you know that bread has alcohol in it?
You wanna join me for a little toast?

Two cannibals were having supper when one said to the other, "You know, I just can't stand my mother-in-law." The second cannibal replied, "Ah, that's all right. Just eat the vegetables."

The farmers are forming a new union; they're going to call it "the E-I-E-I-O"!

My neighbor had beans and pineapples for lunch. I guess he wanted to make Hawaiian music.

One cannibal to another: "So, what's eating you?"

Most people put on weight in certain places. My spouse does it in the dining room.

Did you hear about the potato that went on radio as a newscaster? He was only a common-tater.

I went to the hamburger joint the other day and asked for a large burger and two small fries. The attendant gave me the burger and threw a couple of little kids over the counter.

A cook tried to tell me to cook the cake for only 30 minutes not 60. I didn't go for any of his half-baked ideas.

She was so fat they had to weigh her on the Richter scale.

I love to go into an ice-cream parlor and ask the counter clerk, "Hey, what's the latest scoop?"

I asked for a dozen clams and six oysters at the seafood restaurant. Perhaps I was a little shellfish. But the waiter didn't crab. He said that it was no fluke to order so much fish (so he told the tail). I was not ashamed. No way was I going to flounder in front of him and look stupid. By the way, about my girlfriend: I lobster in the restaurant, but then I flounder.

I spotted Ronald McDonald skinny-dipping at the lake. He was the one with the Sesame Seed Buns.

I like barbecuing. It's the most time I ever spend with my grill friend.

I lost my job at the bakery; the boss claimed I was loafing.

Then I was fired from the orange Juice plant. They said I couldn't concentrate.

I worked for a while at a fish store. I was a herring aid.

A friend asked me to have dinner at a new Japanese restaurant. He said, "Have you every had sushi?". "But of course", I replied, "why, if you knew sushi like I knew sushi, oh, oh, oh what fish!".

I hate to bring this up but dinner was terrible.

He is on a seafood diet. Every time he sees food he eats it.

Everything she eats go to waist.

Her cooking is so bad the flies chipped in to fix the screen door!

I looked for a piece of cake but the table was desserted.

Man walks into a restaurant. He asks the waiter, "What kinds of soup do you have?". The waiter replies, "Well, sir, we have chicken soup and we pea soup." "I'll have chicken soup, please", the customer says. The waiter yells out, "Chicken soup!" "No, wait a minute, I'll have pea soup instead", the man hurries to say. So the waiter yells out, "Hold the chicken make it pea!"

Haiti: Country of coffee drinkers who disdain tea.

Yes, I ate the last remaining fish. I was solely responsible.

Tragedy at the food store. Two employees got sacked.

Trouble at the food processing factory: two employees were canned.

I sat there eating cantaloupe and watching reruns of Lassie... feeling melancholy.

Why don't cannibals eat comedians? They taste funny.

Do Sea Men eat naval oranges?

I wouldn't want to work at a fast-food hamburger joint - they have too high a turnover rate.

When I got hired at my new job they showed me how to make coffee. I asked, "Why do I have to know how to make coffee?"
"Oh, this is just one of the perks," the boss replied.

NASA wants to put a restaurant on the moon but is afraid that it would have no atmosphere.

The students did not like the cafeteria food. They said that they were fed up with it.

I ate eggs Benedict this morning. By the afternoon they had turned on me.

First I wanted pancakes, then I thought about having eggs and bacon.
Yes, I waffled all morning deciding what to eat.

I opened up my paycheck and found parsley in the envelope.
Apparently, my wages had been garnished.

The rabbits ate all the lettuce that I had planted. There was none romaining.

I like to look at cows when we drive out in the country. But they go pasteurize fast.

They fired an executive at the milk processing plant. He was skimming off the top.
When the president found out about it he creamed him.

delicate: a feline that hangs around a sandwich shop.

magazine for gardeners: weeder's digest.

Coach: Son, can you pass this football? Player: Gee, coach, I can barely swallow it!

Two vegetarians in love:
He: "Lettuce elope!"
She: "No, I cantaloupe!"

Vegetarians eschew meat. Is a vegetarian with diarrhea a salad shooter?

castanets: what you need to do first to catch fish.

Bartender sees a grasshopper walk into the bar.
"You know there is a drink named after you?", he says.
"What? Steve?", the grasshopper asks.

I know my supper is ready when the smoke alarm goes off.

Why does Superman like to eat his hamburgers while he is in outer space? Answer: He heard that our there, they are meteor.

Teacher: Give me a sentence with the word, "officiate".
Student: "My dad got sick last night because of a fish he ate."

Good manners advice: Should french fries be eaten with the fingers? Answer: No!
The fingers should be eaten separately.

My silly neighbor planted some Cheerios so he could grow donuts.

My neighbor comes from the town of Donut, Missouri. It's a real hole.

I had supper last night in a restaurant that was so bad, that the other side of the menu was an order blank for a prescription. The mice there were taking Alka Seltzer. When I said to the waiter, "I see you have stew on the menu." So he came over and wiped it off.

PAGE 34

Two friends, a carrot and a potato, were crossing the street. The carrot didn't look and got hit by a truck. The potato rushed his friend to the hospital. After a while, the doctor came out and told the carrot, "Well, I've got some good news and some bad news. The good news is, your friend, the carrot, will make it. The bad news is, he'll be a vegetable the rest of his life."

What are two things you will never have for breakfast? Answer: lunch and supper.

Two peanuts were walking
down the street; one was a-salted.

buccaneer: the high price of corn.

My first girl friend worked at a fast-food hamburger joint: they called her all-beef Patty.

What's that fish doing inside your piano? Answer: "Why, that's my piano tuna."

What's that fish doing in your ear? Answer: "Why, that's my herring aid."

I go fishing just for the halibut. I usually have a whale of a time. I couldn't believe that the captain of the boat worked for scale.

When on vacation, do you ever eat on the road? If yes, be careful you get run over doing that!

Cannibal to other cannibal: "You don't look so well; what's wrong?"
Other cannibal: "Oh, I don't know. I guess I'm just fed up with people."

Why was the cannibal kid kicked out of school? Answer: he was always buttering up the teacher.

How do you recognize rabbit stew? Answer: it has hares in it.

At the check-out counter of the supermarket, I told the check-out girl, "Put this bill on my account...on account of I don't have any money."

New drink: mix prune juice with 7-Up. It's called a hurry-up.

My neighbor used to work in a bubble gum factory, and once he fell into a vat of bubble gum. Boy, did his boss chew him out!

What are the first words at a pickle wedding ceremony? Answer: "Dilly beloved..."

How do you make a hamburger laugh? Answer: you gently pickle it.

What's the difference between buffalos and ice cream cones? Answer: You can't give me a home where the ice cream cones roam.

spectator: potato wearing glasses over its eyes.

I once worked at a seafood restaurant. It was a real dive.

The baker was the breadwinner of the family cause he kneaded the dough.

French cooking is just a lot of crepe.

Do farmers expect the government to bale them out?

Although I am a fungi, there wasn't mushroom on my salad plate.

The imitation butter was only marginal.

ANIMAL JOKES & PUNS

I saw a fly the other day;
I went over to it and said,
"Hey, your person is open."

The depressed man sat in the park petting a duck. I guess he was feeling a little down.

I went over to see the duck show. Only cost me two bills.
I figured that it wouldn't hurt to take a gander.
Who knows? I might even get goosed.

One elephant said to the other after noting the faux pas, "Tusk, tusk".

My dog is so lazy that when she barks she only says, "Bow!".

My friend opened up a combination pet and stereo store last week. He calls it "Woofers and Tweeters".

I once spotted a leopard at the zoo but I really didn't have to, it already was.

Sign on Pet Store: In honor of Mother's Day, all dogs cut in half.

What is black and brown and looks good on a lawyer?
A doberman pincher.

How can you tell the difference between a dead lawyer and a dead dog laying on the road? There are skid marks in front of the dog.

octopus: eight kittens.

toucan: hopefully, if one can't.

It would behoove you to learn more about cows.

I ran over a bird while vacationing in Florida but I have no egrets.

New Chinese cookbook: 101 ways to wok your dog.

hamlet: small pig.

I washed my dog and killed all the bugs that were on her. Now she's ticked off at me.

PAGE 37

My bird bites me when I put my hand in his cage but he never beaks to me.

The NYC library has two large lions in front of it because that way you can read between the lions.

I got a call the other day from an amoeba. He used his cellular phone.

Some daffynitions: Dogma: canine mother. Franchise: food served best with hamburgers. Manatee: a golfer's first position. Paraffin: two sharks swimming.

Everyone made fun of the mock turtle soup.

I have a pet; it's a run-of-the-mill hamster.

I'm no genus at classifying animals.

I went shopping for a fishing rod...the prices made my head reel.

The amoeba was funny but of the one celled organisms, the paramecium was cilia.

Pedicure: What a veterinarian does.

A snake who was employed in show business took his boss to court to demand more pay. But the judge threw the case out. The snake didn't have a leg to stand on.

Why does your new dog wear a Timex on each paw? Answer: because he's a watch dog.

How do you catch a unique bird? Answer: unique up on him.

What do you put on a pig who has poison ivy? Answer: oinkment!

A gorilla was wearing a hearing aid. Now that's unheard of. But she was the gorilla of my dreams!

lionize: what a lion uses to see.

Our neighbors traded in their dogs for other dogs. They were told they should re-woof their house.

Two pigeons were flying over the racetrack. One pigeon says to the other, "I just put everything I had on number 4."

My neighbor opened the door of his Westinghouse refrigerator and found his dog sitting on there. He said, "What are you doing in there?!" The dog replied, "I'm westing."

Billy Bob and Jimmy Jim were fishing on Podunk Lake yesterday. Both men were ecstatic about the large number of Northern trout they were catching. So Billy Bob said to Jimmy Jim, "Golly gee there, Jimmy Jim! We had better remember this spot for when we go fishing next time!" Jimmy Jim replied, "Yep, Billy Bob! Let's take this chalk and mark a big 'X' on the side of this here boat, so that we'll know where this spot is!" Billy Bob then replied, "Why, Jimmy Jim, that is the stupidest idea I ever heard! Why, the next time we go a-fishin', we might not even have the same boat!"

A horse comes into a bar and sits down. The bartender comes over and asks, "So why the long face?"

My pet deer was really lazy today. All she did was lie around. So I fed her something special. Yep, I used yeast to make my doe rise.

What do you call a row of 100 rabbits all stepping backwards? Answer: a receding hare-line.

A man hit a deer on a country road. The sheriff's deputy stopped to write the accident report. He wrote, "leg on road, another leg in ditch, body and two legs under car. Head on showlder of the road. No, schoalder. No, shoawlduh." So he kicks the head to the side and writes, "Head in ditch".

Back in the days of the American Revolutionary War, General George Washington didn't have enough troops to capture the British soldiers near Trenton, New Jersey. So a physicist who joined the Continental Army came to Gen. Washington with an ingenious plan to capture the Tories. The red dye used on the Tory uniforms put out a scent that attracted chickens. So the physicist convinced Gen. Washington that our side could release tens of thousands of chickens surrounding the Tory troops, and as the chickens rushed in to the British encampment, the Tories would have a hard time trying to kick their way out through thousands and thousands of chickens. This military maneuver went down in history to be known as "Chicken Catch a Tory".

My neighbor, a farmer, has a pig with a wooden leg. I asked him how the pig got his wooden leg. He told me, "Well, one day I was changing a tire on my truck when the jack slipped and pinned my leg under the car. Well, my pig came up to me and with his wooden leg he raised the car so that I could get my leg out." I said, "That's quite a story, but it still doesn't explain HOW the pig got the wooden leg." So the farmer continued, "Well, one day I fell asleep on the couch and my cigar fell on the couch and started a fire. My pig smelled the smoke and ran up to the window. He kept tapping on the glass until he woke me and I put out the fire before it spread. My pig thus saved my life!" I replied, "That's a great story! But it still doesn't explain HOW your pig got his wooden leg!" Because of my insistence, the farmer then said to me, "O.K. Here's why my pig has a wooden leg. With a pig that good, you don't just eat him all at once."

My parakeet flew into an electric fan. Too bad, it was shredded tweet.

What do you call a cat who has just walked through the desert? Answer: sandy claws.

It was raining cats and dogs outside today; I know because I stepped in a poodle.

How did the authorities in the shark-attack thriller movie "Jaws" know that the first girl eaten by the great white shark had dandruff? Answer: They found her Head and Shoulders on the beach.

What's red and green and goes 100 miles per hour? Answer: a frog in a blender.

What goes, "Ribbit, ribbit, psssst"? Answer: a frog in a microwave oven.

What's green and goes, "click-click, click-click, click-click"? Answer: a ball-point frog.

Why don't ducks fly upside down? Answer: they don't want to quack up.

Why couldn't the pony sing? Answer: because he had a little colt. Why else couldn't the pony sing? Answer: because he was a little horse.

What do you get if you cross an elephant with a rhino? Answer: El if ino.

How do you make a statue of an elephant? Answer: get a large piece of marble, and then whittle away everything that doesn't look like an elephant.

You know the old saying, "A bird in the hand is useless if you have to blow your nose."

Why do ducks have flat feet? Answer: from stomping out forest fires. Then why do elephants have flat feet? Answer: from stomping out burning ducks.

How do you catch a blue elephant? Answer: with a blue elephant net. Then how do you catch a white elephant? Answer: you hold his tongue till he turns blue, then you catch him with a blue elephant net.

What does a cat say who's been trapped in a refrigerator stuck in cream cheese for three days? Answer: Meow.

What do you get when you cross 100 female pigs with 100 male deer? Answer (say it fast to get the joke): 200 sows and bucks.

What's the last thing to go through a bug's mind when it hits your car's windshield? Answer: its butt.

Two lost hikers in the Alps suddenly saw a large St. Bernard dog approaching them, with a barrel of brandy around his neck. One hiker exclaimed, "Here comes man's best friend!", to which the other hiker added, "Yeah! And look at the big dog bringing it!"

Sir Lancelot the knight ran up to King Arthur to inform him that the queen was kidnapped by soldiers of the enemy army. The king ordered a fresh horse for Lancelot who wanted to go rescue the queen. However, all the horses were being used by the king's knights who were out on patrol. It wa nighttime, dark, dreary, raining very hard and also with a gale blowing. The only animal left for Sir Lancelot to ride on was the king's large St. Bernard. Sir Lancelot exclaimed to the king, "I'll ride your dog to go rescue your Lady!" King Arthur then looked outside at the terrible weather, looked at his dog, and then said to Lancelot, "Nah! I wouldn't send a knight out on a dog like this!"

How do you stop a rhinoceros from charging? Answer: you take away his credit card.

Did you hear about the mother flea who got upset because all her kids were going to the dogs?

How do bunnies get to work? Answer: they ride the Rabbit Transit System.

What's green and goes, "Oink, oink. Oink. oink"? Answer: Porky Pickle.

A kangaroo goes into a bar and orders a 7-up. The bartender says, "Ten dollars. By the way, we don't see many kangaroos here." The kangaroo replies, "At these prices, no wonder!"

Why do seagulls live by the sea? Answer: because if they lived by the bay, they'd be bagels.

What's red and white on the outside, and gray on the inside? Answer: a can of Campbell's cream-of-elephant soup.

What do you get when you cross a skunk with a computer? Answer: a stinking know-it-all.

A trained rabbit became an anesthesiologist. He was known as the Ether Bunny.

What weighs 2000 pounds and comes on a stick? Answer: hippopsicle.

Would you want the egg of a 500-pound canary or the egg of an elephant? I'd prefer the canary. I'm tired of all these elephant yokes.

Some birds have gotten a new canarial disease. But at least there's a tweetment.

A skunk walked into a court room.
The judge yelled, "Odor in the
court, odor in the court!"

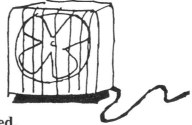

The cow just gave birth. She was decalfenated.

Sign in front of the Veternarian's office: NO LITTERING!

I wanted to buy one bird but ended up with a parakeets.

We could have smoked the meat but it never a cured to us.

Don't hold a frog or you'll get warts....or so I've been toad.

Zebu: what a French ghost says to scare people.

mosquito: small moslem mosque.

What happens when cows laugh? Milk comes out their nose.

I'm watching a movie when I notice that the guy next to me has his dog with him.
The dog laughs at the funny parts of the movie and crys at the sad parts. I am so
amazed at this that I turn to the guy and say, "I can't believe how your dog reacts to
the movie, laughing at the funny scenes and crying at the sad scenes. That is
incredible". "Yes", the man replies "I'm surprised too since he didn't even like the
book!".

GOOD-TASTE RELIGION JOKES & PUNS

A mom heard her young child saying her bedtime prayers, "Give us this day our jelly bread."

Do you know that baseball is mentioned in the Bible? Yes, for the Bible starts out, "In the big inning..."

What is the first miracle mentioned in the Bible?
The first miracle mentioned in the Bible is mentioned in Exodus: It read, "Moses tied his ass to a tree and walked 20 miles."

What is marriage all about? Well, according to the Bible, "Man shall cleave until his wife, and a woman shall cleave unto her husband." Thus, that's what marriage is all about: cleavage.

When I went to the bank to cash a check, the teller told me she was busy, so I should go to the next teller, Ms. Helen Waite. The first teller said to me, "If you want some money, go to Helen Waite."

What did Eve say to Adam? Answer: "I want to turn over a new leaf!"

The Sister asked the class, "Suppose God has a name. Would anyone want to guess what it might be?" One little boy raised his hand and said, "Yes, Sister. I know that his name is Harold." The nun then asks the boy, "Now, Stevie, how do you know that?" "Well," Stevie responds, "we pray like this: 'Our Father, Who art in Heaven, Harold be thy name...'"

As part of the annual Christmas activities at school, the teacher assigned the class to draw their own Christmas cards. All children drew traditional Christmas scenes, but little Tommie drew the manger scene with a big fat man standing with the three kings and the Holy Family. The teacher asked Tommie, "Why, Tommie, describe all those people in your Christmas scene, and who is that big fat man?" Tommie started to describe the picture he drew: "Well, we have Round John Virgin, mother and Child."

How did God stop Adam and Eve from gambling? Answer: He took away their para-dise (pair of dice).

Cannibal to missionary: "So, now I've got you stewing in our pot, and we'll have you for supper!"
Missionary: "Oh, well; it's not a total loss: at least he'll get a taste of religion."

As the airplane was going through very severe turbulence, bouncing all over the place, a minister stood up and said, "I think that now is the time to do something religious. So get out your wallets and pocketbooks because I am going to take up a collection!"

The Pope dies and goes to heaven where he finally meets God. God welcomes him and offers dinner. The Pope is delighted, but is disappointed when he sees only a glass of tomato juice and a stalk of celery on the table. "God, I don't mean to complain", the Pope says, "but I was kind of expecting a little more. After all, this IS heaven." "Yeah, I know", God explains, "but you know how hard it is to cook for two".

A Lutheran dies and goes to heaven. St. Peter escorts him around for a tour of the facilities. "This is the Baptist part of heaven. You can hear the singing from here", St. Paul tells the new heavener. "And this section is for the Jews, and this section is for the Moslems, and then this section over here is for the Lutherans", he continues. "Now as we pass by this next area please be quiet", he tells the new harper. "Why? What is so special about this area", the plucky man asks. "Well, this section is for the Catholics and they think that they are the only ones up here".

"Michaelangelo", the Pope lamented, "next time use a roller!"

Why don't holy rollers have sex standing up? Because they are afraid it will lead to dancing.

My preacher at church is really non-discriminatory. When he hands out the offering plate he accepts all denominations.

The pastor of the church was thankful for the donation of a used organ. First, it was used at a old-time movie theatre, then it was moved to an ice rink. Finally, someone gave it to the church. The pastor thanked God for the organ transplant.

Where did Noah store the bees? In the arc-hives.

If you don't pay your exorcist on time you can get repossessed.

The preacher said, "We need to pray for Mrs. Magilicuti as she has heart problems, and for Mr. Bendix for his lung condition, and for little Michael Harris for his kidney disease". I turned to my wife and commented, "Sounds like an organ recital".

One guys says to his friend, "I just bought a dog but I can't train him".
"No problem. I know someone who can train him in 3 weeks. But I have to tell you, he is a Baptist minister". "Who cares if he is a Baptist minister as long as he can train my dog". So the guy brings his dog to the minister and asks him to train the dog. "Sure thing. You come back in three weeks and you'll see how well trained your dog is!", says the minister. The man comes back in three weeks and sees how the training went. "Sit, boy", he says to the dog and sure enough the dog sits obediently. "Roll over, boy", he says to the dog and sure enough the dog rolls over. "Heal, boy", he says to the dog whereupon the dog puts his paw on his master's head!

heretic: insect found on a sheepdog.

Sign in front of church: We will not be undersouled!

Jews and Christians alike admire Moses. This is the first case of prophet-sharing mentioned in the Bible.

The minister was a pitcher in the co-ed church league. When a woman stood at the plate, he could throw it right pastor.

The smell of the sandlewood left me incensed.

Nuns inhabit a convent.

Ornamentally, we have tinsel and colored lights on our Christmas tree.

Awake: see funeral.

To open up the church door Friar Tuck used his monkey.

Aspire: the structure on the top of the church.

The little girl was sitting with her parents in church when suddenly she felt sick. "Dad," she said, "I think I'm going to be throw up!" Her father said to her, "Quickly! Run to the back of the church, go into the vestibule, then down the stairs, turn to the right and then run down the hallway, and you'll find the little girl's restroom. Hurry!" So the little girl ran to the back of the church but came back only a half-minute later. Her dad, surprised, asked her, "Didn't you make it in time?" The little girl replied, "Well, I started to go where you told me to, but once I got into the vestibule I noticed this little brown box attached to the wall, and the writing on it said, 'For the sick'".

PETE'S POETRY SAMPLER

"A SCHMIBBER MET A PLIBBER"

A schmibber met a plibber by the crooked, winding schmee.
The plibber had a blaffer with a rugged hoarhadee.
The schmibber found a gobbmer underneath a silly ghree.
The schmibber told the plibber to jablon a boonafee.

And then a glubber-falbner found forgotten flibbelflash.
Forgotten faltoe-finletter found famous frombahash.
Brainy broomlah brian brought banjo-banner from grayton.
While woygie wensis la-la ate an onion by the sun.

And if you are a-wondering what this yarn is all about,
All you hafta do is open your big mouth and shout:
"A schmibber met a plibber by the crooked, winding schmee.
The plibber asked the schmibber, 'Woygie onion brainy-dee?' "

"THE VILLAGE KISS"

In Greenwich Village I met a girl
Who seemed to like my looks.
So when I asked her for a kiss,
She gave me one that went like this:

Uh smooch, uh smooch, uh stoopchee pwuh.
"Oh I like that, dear girl", I uttered,
So to my lips she just rebuttered:

Uh smooch, uh smooch, uh stoopchee pwuh.
"Ah girl, what you have done to me
Can best be expressed rapidly:

"Uh smooch, uh smooch, uh stoopchee pwuh."

"FILTHY DIRT"

Dirty dirt and filthy filth*
Cross them, yes you do*
We now get dirty filthy dirt*
And filthy dirty too.

"DO YOU LIKE TO GET UP IN THE MORNING, MARY BROWN?"

Do you like
To get up
In the morning,
Mary Brown?

Yes, I like
To get up
In the morning,
Talking Rooster.

"WHERE THERE MAY BE A POOR MAN"

I want to live
Where there may be a man
Without any riches
That I may not have.

A man in whose home
A door may be found
Unloosened at one end
So it may be used.

A door which is wood
That had come from a tree
Which was felled by an axe
That had also some wood.

An axe that was made
By a man from this house
Where I want to live
With those riches of his.

"A POEM"

Hello to you today.
Today to you hello.
To you, today, hello.
Hello today to you.

"NOODLE-DEE-DOODLE"

Galileo used his noodle;
Isaac Newton, noodle-dee-doodle.

"FLOATING DOWN THE RIVER IN MINE COFFIN"

Wandering waters of pestulence patience,
Pondering proudly their whispery work,
Carry a visitor haplessly drifting,
Softly yet swiftly, this Stanislaw Kirk.

Poor Stanislaw, Stanislaw, whithre are ye drifting,
Ye dead gruesome shell of original man?
The liquid ye sail on fears even thy coffin
That floats on the foam of this bubbling sea.

Lo, Night hast arrived as thine dear man departs;
He floats in his coffin down the Missouri River.

"EXCESSIVE SENSES"

One may shelter a dog from the cold.
The dog may be big, as big as a ball.
The ball was not here, for it is a dog.
Thus, there is no dog at all.

To shelter the dog, yes, from the cold,
It must be cold or there is no reason.
There is no reason, so there is no cold.
With no cold we need not a shelter, that is true.

"GNATS"

Oooe!, Gnats!
Oooe!, Gwhere?
Oooe!, Ghere!

"THE AIRPLANE IN THE WELL"

Chapter 1: The Letter in the Mailbox

Sounds of stirring silence or perhaps of a haircut rushed up over the Earth as a day dawned. Who could it be who would stare at the heavens at this early hour? Yep, you guessed it, it was Peter. Natch this is not an unusual situation because today is something special. You see, today Peter is going to the big city.

He skipped across the room with a smile. He noticed that his wife was still sleeping, so he cautiously kept his silence. His wife, though, woke up. "Want some popcorn?", she asked.

Putting on his rectangular pants and olive-colored hat, Peter proceeded to leave his house. However, before leaving, he stared at his overcoat hanging in the closet and exclaimed to his wife, "It's gray!"

Somewhere in a tree outside, a canary tweeted.

Chapter 2: Chocolate Cake

Out under the outside sky, Peter walked to the gate of the big city. He smiled appreciatively as he thought of the mess he had left back home. Once in the big city, he soon learned to stick out his thumb and get a ride.

Eventually, Peter found himself in a park. As he walked among the outstretched arms of the glistening trees and listened to the symphony of the birds, he began to feel alone. Wanting company, Peter ran.

Thenst it was that he discovered it: the mighty river, flowing wet through all these years, uninterrupted by rain and storm. Here he met Margie. "Want some popcorn?", she asked.

Now night was arriving. Stranded in a big city, Peter became frightened! In a fit of terror he tore through the streets, rushing for the airport! He got on a plane and it crashed in a well.

DOCTOR JOKES & PUNS

Anyone who goes to a psychiatrist should have his head examined.

I went to my doctor to complain about the ringing in my ear. I said, "Doctor, doctor, I have this continuous ringing in my ear!" The doctor said, "Don't answer it."

The doctor said to my neighbor, "You're gonna live to be 60." My neighbor told the doctor, "But I AM 60!" The doctor replied, "See, I told ya!"

My next door neighbor went to his doctor with this complaint: "Doctor, my love-life is terrible!" His doctor gave him this advice: "Take off 20 pounds and run 10 miles a day. Then come back to see me in one week." So, one week later, my neighbor telephones his doctor. The doctor asks, "So, how's your love life?" My neighbor replies, "I don't know. I'm 70 miles away!"

My neighbor asked his doctor after his physical exam was over, "Well, doc, how do I stand?" The doctor replied, "That's what puzzles me."

Man goes to a psychiatrist. The psychiatrist says to him, "You're crazy!" The man says, "I want a second opinion" So the psychiatrist says, "O.K., you're ugly too!"

Doctor to patient: "I hate to tell you this, but you have only six months to live."
Patient: "Doc, I hate to tell you this, but I don't have any money to pay you.
Doctor: "In that case, you've got six additional months to live!"

Man to psychiatrist: "Nobody wants to talk with me!"
Psychiatrist: "Who's the next patient?"

A doctor fell down the well on his rural homestead. His wife ran out and heard him yelling for help. She looked down and scolded her husband, "Doctor, doctor, don't you know that you're supposed to take care of the sick first, and then the well?"

Does a proctologist practice holistic medicine?

"Doctor, doctor! My friend swallowed a pen!"
Doctor: "Then use a pencil."

Doctor to nurse; "How's the patient who swallowed a quarter?" Nurse: "No change yet."

This guy comes into the doctor's office and says, "Doc, I have a real problem. Just two drops of liquor and I start giving my money away." "That's too bad," said the doctor, "Why don't we talk about this problem over a few drinks."

This lady goes to a psychiatrist and says, "Doctor, my husband's got a problem For the past six months he's thought that he is a chicken!" The doctor asks her, "Why didn't you send him to me earlier?" She relies, "I would have, but we needed the eggs."

What did one chromosome say to the other chromosome? Answer: "Nice genes you're wearing."

How do you tell the male chromosome from the female chromosome? Answer: pull down its genes.

My neighbor's dentist is so near-sighted that instead of putting his drill into his patients' mouths, he sometimes sticks his drill into their noses; he now has a sign over his worksite to remind him to do the right thing: "Don't stick you business into other people's noses!"

A lady went to a psychiatrist. "Doctor," she cried, "you've got to help me! My husband thinks he's a refrigerator!" The doctor asks, "So what's wrong with that?", to which the lady replies, "Most of the time it's okay, but when he falls asleep at night with his mouth open, that darn light keeps me awake!"

A doctor tried to convince his patient about the evils of drinking too much alcohol. "When you drop a live worm into a glass of water, what happens?", he asked. The patient replied, "He swims around." "Right!", said the doctor. "Now when you drop a live worm into a glass of wine, what happens?" "He dies", said the patient. "Right! When you drop a live worm into a glass of whiskey, what happens?" "He dies", said the patient. "Right again", said the doctor. "So what lesson have you learned from this?" asked the doctor. The patient replied, "If you drink alcohol, you'll never have worms!"

I don't think my doctor's any good; all his patients are sick.

At the proctologists convection the opening speaker raised his glass, toasted the audience and said, "Bottoms up!"

A proctologist and a psychiatrist shared an office. They called it odds and ends.

A dentist really manages a filling station.

I had to stop using a urinal since my hernia operation. The doctor told me not to lift any heavy objects.

At the pharmaceutical agency they were experimenting with rabbits for a cure for baldness. It was a hare raising experiment.

My doctor specializes in eyes, ears, nose, throat and wallet.

Definition of middle age: when getting up out of an easy chair is considered weight lifting.

My dentist told me that I needed to have a bridge put in. I told him, "Let's cross that when we get to it". So he crowned me instead.

j

My doctor told the patient that part of his colon would have to be removed. The patient was worried that he'd be left with only a semicolon.

The doctor told me that I had to have an operation to have my appendix out. I couldn't afford the operation so I asked him if he could just retouch the x-ray.

A pediatrician is a doctor with little patients.

The medical doctor came into the bar everyday at seven and always asked for a walnut daiquiri. One day the bar tender told the M.D., "Sorry, sir but we have no walnuts today. Can I get you a Hickory Daiquiri, Doc?".

My wife has laryngitis but its nothing to speak of.

The man next door finally got rid of the bugs on his scalp but he got a ticket from the local cops for driving without head lice.

Secretary: Doctor, there is a man in the waiting room who claims he is invisible.
Doctor: Tell him I can't see him right now.

Brace Yourself: Title of Time-Life Do it Yourself Orthodontistry book.

I wanted to have a treatment by the acupuncturist but was shocked by the sticker price.

I wanted to be an apprentice for an acupuncturist since I was offered on the jab training.

The dermatologist makes rash decisions. I was itching to tell you that!

Man at bar: Give me a glass of prune juice.
Bartender: Is that for here?
Man at bar: No, it's to go.

My brother just quit his job of serving patients at a mental institution. He got tired of serving soup to nuts.

I had a weak back about a week back. My wife had a weak ego about a week ago.

Do optometrists see eye to eye?

Do chiropractors rub people the wrong way?

Do allergists look down their nose on people?

The dentist fell in love with his patient ever since he worked on her abscessed tooth. Just goes to show that abscesses make the heart grow fonder.

The foot doctor discovered a way to control athlete's foot.
It was a pedicure.

Varicose veins: Veins that are too close to one another.

Outpatient: A person that has fainted.

I went to the eye doctor just the other day. He was dilated to see me. Apparently, I was his brightest pupil.

dilate: postponed telephone call

The proctologist is operating and whispers to his nurse. She runs out and brings back a cold beer. The doctor says, "No, No! I said butt light.
The man complained of having dreams of talking mice, talking dogs and talking ducks. "Don't worry", said the psychiatrist, "you are just having Disney spells".

From the moment the doctor cauterize, he knew he loved her!

Sign in optometrist's office: If you don't see what you're looking for, you've come to the right place.

physician: a person who makes soft drinks.

"Do you want more food?", asked the waiter to the pregnant woman.
"No", she replied, "I gestate".

A lady goes up to the pharmacist and hands him her prescription.
"You have to be careful with this medicine, it has codeine in it. It can be habit forming", the pharmacist says to her.
"Don't be ridiculous!", she says, "I've been taking it for years".

After he caught his foot
on the fence, he walked
with a gate.

liverwurst: assessment of an alcoholic's liver.

Women deliver their babies on Labor Day.

The judge got food poisoning on account of the mediate.

There was the faint smell of ether in the air.

He was hit in the butt by a bicycle which nearly rectum for life.

pillow: medicine on the floor.

secure: when the ocean heals.

strychnine: an emphatic "NO" in German.

He stopped smoking just in the nicotine.

My chiropractor spent some time in the joint.

I got sick while visiting France; it must have been a Paris site.

SLIGHTLY NAUGHTY JOKES & PUNS

A woman was taking her husband
to court as he was so stingy he
wouldn't give her money to buy a
new bra. She was suing him for
lack of support.

My friend is so lazy he married a pregnant woman.

One snake said to the other, "This place is really the pits, we don't have a pot to hiss in."

I don't enjoy listening to orchestral music. Too much sax and violins.

Did you hear about the Indian who won the tea drinking contest and later on in his tee pee?

With two pairs of pants drooping down around his knees, the scraggly man walked into the bar. At that moment the bar tender looked at him and said, "Hey buddy, what you need is a couple of belts".

We heard that the owner of the fast-food hamburger joint was caught skinny-dipping. He was the one with the Sesame Seed Buns. Actually, he had to quit skinny-dipping; he just couldn't bare it anymore.

The milkman stopped by the young lady's house to pick up her milk bottles. He noticed a note in one bottle. It read "Please leave 40 bottles of milk tomorrow". He thought that the note might be a joke so he knocked on the door to verify it. The cute young girl came to door. "Miss, do you really want 40 bottles of milk tomorrow?", the milkman asked.
"Yes, I do. You see I bathe in it since it is good for my skin", she replied.
"Do you want it pasteurize?", the milkman chariot.
"No, just past my shoulders", she said.

shampoo: fake dog droppings.

An older lady confided in her friend. "Clara", she said, "I hate to admit it but here I am at 65 and I'm having my first affair."
"Well, I'm happy for you Helen", her friend replied, "who's the caterer?"

A girl at the office said, "I went to the Virgin Islands".
"Oh, yeah", I said, "what did you come back as?"

That pile of doo-doo near the piano must be Beethoven's third movement.

We had to remove the Air Force stickers that were in the men's room. AIM HIGH is not a good motto to display over the urinals.

What do you call a woman who has PMS and ESP? A bitch who knows everything.

The EPA thought that the Great Lakes were polluted so they took a Huron sample.

Wisconsin license plate: Come smell our dairy-aire!

"You are a selfish man", said the Judge to the defendant. "It is against the law to be married to two woman!", he continued.
The man looked up at the judge perplexed, "Selfish? I thought it was bigamy".

My friend has a job at a panty hose factory. He pulls down about 40,000 a year.

German word for constipation: Farfrumpoopen.

I think that bird wants to buy your car. He left a deposit.

My next door neighbor was sitting in her chair with not a stitch of clothing on! So I yelled at her, "Hey, put something on!" She yelled back, "I can't! The TV's broken!"

Two pigeons were flying over the racetrack. One pigeon says to the other, "I just put everything I had on number 4."

A mommy is trying to get her 4-year old son to stop sucking his thumb. So she tells him, "If you keep sucking your thumb, you'll get bigger and bigger and bigger and then you will burst!" That afternoon, while riding with his mom on a city bus, the boy spots a woman who is nine-months pregnant. He taps her on the shoulder and then yells out, "I know what you've been doing!"

My neighbor accidentally stabbed himself on the antenna of his new van. Too bad, because he got van-aereal disease.

I once started a toilet paper factory but I got wiped out. Scott was after my butt.

Then there's this husband and wife team who are so unromantic that they call their water bed, "Lake Placid".

Give me a sentence with the word "pencil" in it. Answer: "If you don't wear a belt, your pencil fall down!"

Don't make love in a buggy, 'cause horses carry tails.

PAGE 57

I once dated a girl who worked for Kodak. She was underexposed and overdeveloped.

When someone accuses you of being naughty, just them him or her, "I deny the allegation and defy the alligator!"

What did the well-endowed soused woman have on the morning after New Year's Eve? Answer: three hang-overs.

Mary had a little lamb. The doctor was surprised.

Jack and Jill went up the hill to fetch a pail of water. They didn't come down for two or three hours...I guess they didn't go for water.

My neighbor went into an elevator and encountered a totally naked woman. He said to her, "You know, my wife has an outfit just like that!"

Is dancing an asset to music?

Zebra: the largest one they make.

He asked the young redhead at the party, "Do you want to play Zip Code with me?"
"What kind of game is that?", she replied.
"Well, it is a lot like post office but much faster!".

I went to the car parts store and went up to the young female attendant asking to see her headlights. She took her shirt off! So I stood there beaming at her.

I once knew a librarian. She was so cute I asked if I could take her out for an overnight loan.

His wife was such a bad lover, after sex he didn't know whether to embrace her or embalm her.

I always try to grab the gusto...but last time I tried it I got slapped.

So I asked the young woman if she could play golf.
"Sure, I love it!", she replied.
"Great, how about playing around with me?", I asked.

I went out with a loose woman. On our first date her arm fell off.

A guy comes home and sees his wife packing her suitcase.

"Where are you going?", he asks her.

"Well, I found out that I could make $100.00 a night in Las Vegas doing what I do for you for free! So I am moving!", she shouts back.

Moments later the husband starts packing.

"Where are you going?", she asks him.

"I'm following you to Las Vegas to see how you are going to live on $200.00 a year!", he replies.

When I went to college my mother told me to sow my wild oats. So I went to the Agriculture School.

I have started to take Vitamin E pills to enhance my virility. Yesterday I accidentally dropped the pills in the toilet. Now I can't get the seat to go down!

Did you hear about the woman that backed into an airplane propeller?
Dis-as-ter.

JUST PLAIN SILLY JOKES & PUNS

A snake who was employed in show business took his boss to court to demand more pay. But the judge threw the case out. The snake didn't have a leg to stand on.

BULLETIN!: A man just fell off the World Trade Center, falling over 110 stories. Miraculously, he was not even hurt! When interviewed, he revealed that he was wearing his light fall suit.

We just heard about the sad ink-spot. His brother was in the pen and had a long sentence.

Are you a safe driver? Isn't it monotonous driving a safe?

Why do we drive on parkways and park on driveways?

Why does a car deliver a shipment, and a ship deliver cargo?

Why is it better to buy a thermometer in the winter than in the summer? Answer: in the summer, it's higher.

What do you call a girl who has three boyfriends all named William? Answer: a Bill collector.

What's black and white and lives in the Tropics? Answer: a lost penguin.

Did you hear about the Texan who put ice-cream on his head? He wanted to "Remember the A-la-mode."

Why, when the lady clapped her hands, did they make the sound, "clang, clang, clang" instead of "clap, clap, clap"? Answer: because she had dish-pan hands.

Some less-than-brilliant people froze to death at the drive-in theater. They went to see, "Closed for the Winter".

A drunk puts a dime into the parking meter and the needle goes to 60. "Uh, oh," he says, "I just lost 100 pounds!"

When George Washington was campaigning for president, his wife, Martha, was always following him around and she was carrying a bucket. It seems that even back in those days, there were leaks coming out of Washington.

The post office is adding more digits to your zip code. Too much of the mail was getting through.

My neighbor threw firecrackers on the kitchen floor. He wanted to see Linoleum Blown-apart.

This guy comes into the doctor's office and says, "Doc, I have a real problem. Just two drops of liquor and I start giving my money away." "That's too bad," said the doctor, "Why don't we talk about this problem over a few drinks."

A pebble went to the rock concert, but he was the smallest one there.

Why does the postal service charge 32 cents to mail a letter? Answer: 20 cents to mail it and 12 cents for storage.

The city of Fairbanks, Alaska now has parka meters.

A young lady was applying for her first secretarial job. In the job interview, the personnel clerk told her, "Well, this job pays $300 a week, but in six months the pay is $350." "Fine," said the applicant, "I'll come back in six months."

You ought to be on the stage. There's one leaving in an hour.

A sixth-grader came home with his report card which showed an A in spelling, an A in reading and an A in grammar. The mom knew her son wasn't that bright, so she went to visit the teacher. She told him, "You know, I'm not complaining that my son has straight A's in English, but I know he can't write well, he doesn't know how to spell big words, and he can't even express himself in a full sentence." The teacher replied to her, 'Oh well, that don't matter none nohow."

During the Christmas holidays, a golfer hits his golf ball into the woods where it bounces off a quail. The golfer exclaims, "Wow! a partridge on a par three!"

My friend checked his family tree and found out he was the sap.

Two trees were trying to do their algebra homework. One tree says to the other, "This problem has me stumped."

Knock, knock!
Who's there?
Isabel.
Isabel who?
Isabel out of order?

In northern Wisconsin, it's nine months of winter and three months of bad sledding.

There are only two seasons in northern Wisconsin: winter and road construction.

We wrote down our best jokes and then threw the papers into the fireplace...and the fire just roared and roared!

In the Ozark Mountains of southern Missouri, explorers have just found the last undiscovered Indian tribe. There were only 500 of them left, and they all shared the same physical deformity: they all had no nipples! So, since the discoverers found them, they could name them. They called the tribe, "the Indian-nipple-less 500".

I used to work for a company that manufactured bullets. Yeah, I was a big shot. Unfortunately, they fired me.

What's a hoola hoop with a nail it in? Answer: a navel destroyer.

An insult: "What do you think of the human race? I'd like the opinion of an outsider."

I read the obituary page in the newspaper today. Did you know that everybody died in alphabetical order?

Time to check the temperature outside. Let's check with Arthur. Arthur mometer.

My uncle's name was Ferdinand and my aunt's name was Liza, so they named my cousin Fertilizer.

If every person in this country had a pink automobile, then we'd be known as a pink car nation.

What did one casket say to the other casket? Answer: "Ahem. Is that you coffin?"

The nearby movie theater is showing a double feature this weekend, two disaster flicks: "Earthquake" and "The Towering Inferno". It was billed as "shake and bake."

I like California despite all its faults.

I took all my money out of the bank; I just lost interest in it.

If you throw salt on your neighbor's car battery, you could be charged with a salt and battery.

In New Mexico, we often have Apache ground-fog; in Arizona, it's possible to observe an approaching squaw-line.

What is "ALOHA"? Answer: someone who laughs quietly.

What happened when Beethoven died? Answer: he decomposed.

If Thomas Edison hadn't perfected using electricity, we'd be watching television and playing our VCRs by candlelight!

The lost Heckawe Tribe was wandering through the forest, chanting, "We're the Heckawe!"

What TV show reminds you of a mother rocking her baby to sleep? Answer: Eyewitness Snooze.

Professional baseball players are NOT stupid! A recent survey shows that about 90 percent of them got straight A's in school. And now that they're in the work force, they'll learn the rest of the alphabet.

A drunk staggered into a bar, shouting, "Happy New Year, everybody!" The people told him that it was the middle of March. "Yikes!," exclaimed the drunk, "My wife's gonna kill me! I've never been this late before!"

Did you hear about the rope trick? No? Then skip it!

My co-writer's jokes are so bad, that when I was telling mine, the audience was still booing his jokes during my act.

Of what use is a pill that's half-aspirin and half-glue? Answer: it's used for a splitting headache.

Who is the smallest soldier in the army? Answer: the soldier who fell asleep on his watch.

On Halloween, the near-sighted ghosts wear spooktacles.

What are "mixed emotions"? Answer: watching your mother-in-law drive off a cliff in your brand new car.

Definition of "baloney": from the bottom of the foot up towards the knee.

I don't know if its true that the ship that brought Count Dracula to England was a blood vessel.

It was so cold today that the lawyers were keeping their hands in their OWN pockets!

The boxer was knocked down. The count was being yelled, "one...two...three...four...". The boxer's coach yelled, "Don't get up until eight!' The boxer replied, "Duh, what time is it now?"

Guy: "Have you seen a cop around?"
Other guy: "I haven't seen a cop for 5 or 6 blocks."
Guy: "In that case, stick 'em up!"

How does an Eskimo keep his house together? Answer: He uses igloo.

What's the definition of "debate". Answer: it's de ting dat you put on de end of de fish hook.

A reporter left the nuclear power plant and gave a glowing report.

I took my umbrella to work and it started to rain. When I opened it, it was full of holes so I got wet. My co-worked said to me, "Why did you take the umbrella with the holes in it?" I told him, "I didn't think it was going to rain."

Why is April 1st a day of rest? Answer: because it follows a March of 31 days.

What's the difference between a bus driver and a kleenex? Answer: One knows his stops and the other stops his nose.

Which is the strongest day of the week? Answer: Sunday, because all the rest are week-days.

Two astronauts were in orbit on a space shuttle. One of them goes outside for a space walk. About an hour later, the outside astronaut knocks on the spacecraft's door. The other astronaut asks, "Who's there?"

In a crowd I suddenly felt somebody's hand entering my back pocket where my wallet was. I caught the perpetrator and said, "Just what do you think you're doing?" He said, "Why, I'm just looking for a dollar." I replied, "Then why didn't you ask me?" He then said, "I don't talk to strangers."

We went to separate schools together.

What gets bigger the more you take out of it?
Answer: a hole.

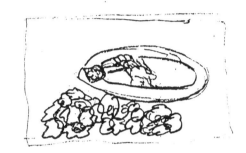

What's round and has two sides? Answer: a circle; it has an inside and an outside.

My neighbor gets so many parking tickets that the police department just issued him a season's ticket.

mummy: an Egyptian pressed for time and kept under wraps.

Tourist to local person: Have you lived your whole life here?
Local person: No, not yet.

A lady had two tattoos on her knees. She had the devil tattooed on one knee and fire on the other. When she crossed her legs, it looked like hell.

Neighbor: "I do all my wash in Tide."
Me: "Why?"
Neighbor: "It's too cold out-tide."

A politician who slings mud, loses ground.

Bumper sticker in braille: "If you can read this, you're too darn close!"

My next door neighbor just invented unscented perfume.

Why did the skeleton refuse to ride the roller coaster? Answer: no guts!

I was walking down the street today when suddenly the prescription on my eyeglasses ran out.

We two writers of this book stayed up all last night to see where the sun went when it set. And then it dawned on us!

My neighbor is such a procrastinator, that he received his belly button at age 12.

What do you get when you cross the Lone Ranger with a Q-tip? Answer: kemo-swabi.

Want to have some fun? Enter an antiques store and ask, "What's new?"

It was so hot out today I saw two trees fighting over a dog.

It was so cold out today I saw a male dog stuck to a fire hydrant.

Our mailman is too old for his job. He lost a little bit of his zip.

I like our new mailman. He carries his job out to the letter.

The interior decorator wanted eight shelves not six for his book collection. Seemed to me that he was a little shelfish.

A ghost that doesn't scare anyone any more doesn't Caribou.

A sign in front of the mortuary said, "Join our funeral plan now! We'll be the last ones to let you down."

The beauty shop had a catchy slogan that said, "If your hair isn't becoming to you, you ought to be coming to us".

One elephant said to the other after noting the faux pas, "Tusk, tusk".

Ground up kelp from the ocean is said to be good for you. I guess that it is a new form of Vitamin Sea.

The course that I took on river flooding was over my head. Left me high and dry. The instructor had a punk hair style. I guess he was new wave.

That sports car is a Porsche excuse for a car.

I have a new foreign car. It is called a Ronzoni. It Runzoni if you push it.

The more I study vectors the tensor I get.

Replacing fluorescent fixtures is really light work.
I told that to our repairman at work and he blew his fuse.

Did you hear about the father who spent a fortune sending his football-playing son to college. All he got was a quarterback.

My friend was a great violin player but had to quit after 5 years. He was all strung out.

I went over to the sales clerk holding
a pair of suspenders and said, "This
is a hold up".

Sign on Swimming Pool store: Save Big Money on Our Liquidation Sale!

The PBS station had a special on the danger of flash floods. I didn't understand it. Most of the material was over my head.

A guy named Ben takes a shower, steps out and uses an electric shaver and electrocutes himself. They cremate his body and put him in a jar. Morale: a Benny shaved is a Benny urned.

Do Eskimos keep their houses together with igloo?

My podiatrist is a callous man.

Sign by a music store: Took our Chopin Listz, Bach in a Minuet.

Genealogy: Study of Barbara Eden.

cabbage: how old you have to be to drive a taxi.

Most people were scared by the tsunami but he thought that it was swell.

Yes, I ate the last remaining fish. I was solely responsible.

taboo: why ghosts go out at night.

Don't ever forget what your teacher torture.

He wanted to buy the Indian carvings but he didn't know how to totem home.

The electrician's fears were not grounded.

I couldn't sleep under the stars due to the noise in the Sonoran Desert.

I had a flat while driving my car to work. I decided to retire.

I am not good at flying. I prefer Terra Firma. The more firma the less terra.

One of the Olympic sledders was disqualified for being a sore lugger.

Have you ever seen a bathroom sink?

The shoe store salesmen were a couple of loafers.

Why do some communities write "Slow Children" on the street?
Is that anything to be proud of?

The blacksmith signed the check and was charged with forgery.

I don't know much about the islands in the Pacific atoll.

The judge handed the thief a light sentence of three years in prism.

The music teacher was removed from the staff for not teaching with notes.

We decided to move from New York City to Salem, Oregon. I guess we settled on an Oregon transplant.

The secretary filed her nails last Tuesday and still can't find them.

Two banana peels make
an excellent pair of slippers.

I gave my students a pop quiz. I asked them what their father's first name was.

Popsicle: My father's bike.

Varicose veins: Veins that are too close to one another.

Artist's conception: a baby.

As a CPA I tried to move the accounts around but I couldn't budget.

The prospective cheerleader got the job since he had a leg up on the competition.
Did you know that the inventor of the door knocker got the Nobel prize?

I was asked to help sell Christmas trees so before I left the house I got spruced up.

I believe she practiced palm reading for her hobby or something along those lines.

I have a Superior knowledge of the Great Lakes. Isn't that a little Erie? I am not
putting Huron, either.

The lightning specialist died of a stroke.

My friend works at a candle store. He is at wicks ends! At first business was great
but now it has tapered off.

Did you hear that the treasury department employees want to go on strike. They
want to make less money.

NASA wants to put a restaurant on the moon but is afraid that it would have no
atmosphere.

I was thrown out of the concert hall because I didn't conduct myself.

He: "So, I'll pick you up for our date at 8 o'clock. What's your address?"
She: "I live on Twain Street."
He: "O.K., what number?"
She: "Twenty-two."
He: "O.K., so I'll pick you up at eight at two-two Twain."

She didn't know what color to pick. Blue, red, green, fusche.
So she decided to go back to the fusche.

Name of company whose job it is to knock down monuments: Edifice Wrecks!

The oil companies don't hire people unless they are doing well.

I asked for the shoe shine man to shine my boots, but I was rebuffed.

Customer: Do you like your job cleaning chimneys?
Chimney sweep: Oh yes, it soots me fine!

What happens when the smog clears over California? UCLA

Why did Cleopatra refuse to accept that Mark Anthony had left her?
She was Queen of Denial.

Sign in Pool store: Come to our liquidation sale!

Sign in Hot Air balloon store: Buy now before inflation!

Did Tennessee the same thing that Arkansas? Guess Alaska and find out what
Juneau.

The painter drank more and more turpentine until he simply varnished into thinner.

I went into the message pallor but was disappointed to find it was self-service.

Euphrates River? No, I swim in it all the time.

I went shopping for a fishing rod...the prices made my head reel.

What's a metaphor if you can't use it?

Did Adam and Eve have belly-buttons?

Not all the airports in Idaho are small potatoes. At least one of their cities is usually Boise.

Air bags for new cars are
sold at inflated prices.

tear gas: produced by eating onions and beans.

migraine: what a farmer says to himself while he overlooks his wheat crop.

terrain: What we need in order to have the flowers and trees grow.

channel surfing: what you do when you are not remotely interested in a TV program.

He fell into the cesspool and was interred.

Junior: Mommy why is Grandpa reading the Bible?
Mommy: He studying for finals.

She used to work at Victoria's secret, but they gave her the pink slip.

I used to eat a lot of ham. Now I am cured.

paradigm: 20 cents.

"Do you do weight lifting?"
"Yes, I work with a couple of dumb bells at work!"

I looked at all the colors the artist was painting but
found none palatable.

When Hurricane Fran hit North Carolina, she caused so much flash flooding that the flood
waters spilled over into Virginia. Many residents of Virginia then complained about being
exposed to second-hand flood.

At the dog show I was the first one to spot the Dalmation.

She looked behind her in the produce section of the store and there he was again. Yes, she was being stalked.

The fact that he had skin-dived to 1000 feet was difficult to fathom.

euthanasia: children living in China.

intense: where campers usually sleep.

When I get sick in an airport, I worry about it being a terminal disease.

The yard was buzzing with excitement. All the insects knew what katydid.

The BMWs were selling fast in Germany since the price had been marked down.

The Indian woman's outfit was a sari excuse for a dress.

How do you clean a watch? With dial soap.

The dizzy blonde was excited by faint praise.

converse: poems penned by a prisoner.

The chasm where the beautiful blonde had fallen was drop dead gorges.

The two guitarists were arguing over how to play discord.

The two singers tried to harmonize but they couldn't duet.

Pollution is the price we pay for living in an effluent society.

cryptic: sound of a clock in a tomb.

escape: the red cloak that superman wears.

The Frenchman wore the silly hat even though his friends bereted him.

She recorded too many people living in one house. She obviously had taken leave of her census.

I get tense while conjugating verbs.

In his army clothes he looked fatigued.

PAGE 72

futile: what is left over after putting in a bathroom floor.

The wedding gift was meant fortuitous.

hexagon: canceled spell.

I inspected the starboard, port, stern and keel of the boat. Yep, I looked over the hull thing.

"I hate this pineapple", Tom said dolefully.

She fashioned hirsute out of mohair.

They paid him tribute in a laud voice.

He apparently jumped off the building, or so it was a ledged.

Taking your clothes off in a public place is not a lewd.

I wish I could finish furniture like she does, but I lacquer dedication.

I fretted about singing the song but for naught. I had no treble with it at all!

tutor: another name for a car horn.

Sign near poolside: Plenty of room in pool for swimming! No Wading!

The Democrats and Republicans are incongruous.

infantry: a sapling.

The Scottish man on an outfit I would have kilt for.

hyperbola: an excited bowler.

George Washington was the only president to be drawn and then quartered.

Crystals can be bought in quartz containers.

rawhide: child's butt after spanking.

realize: opposite of fake lies.

When I couldn't find the paper stock the manager reamed me out.

rebate: what you need to do when the first worm wiggles off the hook.

recede: what you need to do in the fall to improve your lawn.

regale: another gust of wind.

He won every forecasting contest. He was the raining champion.

repeal: act of ringing the church bells one more time.

The jeweller had fixed many watches in his day. He looked forward to retirement and a chance to unwind.

Although the American had studied in France, he never got over Cs.

He had to work three jobs, owing to his casino bills!

knapsack: a bed for a toddler.

I opened the door to the tower to let the bats in the bell free.

Sign in front of flowering bush: Please Don't Peonies.

Poached Eggs: eggs stolen from the henhouse.

Polite: flashlight on a chain.

I saw the rug maker looming in the distance.

pungent: a man who tells puns.

Gymnasts form the pyramid with three people at the bottom while the rest just pylon.

The palm reader could not prophet from her work.